Everything You'll Ever Need

You Can Find Within Yourself

CHARLOTTE FREEMAN

THOUGHT
CATALOG
Books

THOUGHTCATALOG.COM
NEW YORK · LOS ANGELES

THOUGHT
CATALOG
Books

Published by Thought Catalog Books, an imprint of the digital magazine Thought
Catalog, which is owned and operated by The Thought & Expression Company
LLC, an independent media organization based in Brooklyn, New York and Los
Angeles, California.

This book was produced by Chris Lavergne and Noelle Beams. Art direction and
design by KJ Parish. Special thanks to Bianca Sparacino for creative editorial direc-
tion and Isidoros Karamitopoulos for circulation management.

Visit us on the web at thoughtcatalog.com and shopcatalog.com.

Made in the United States of America.

ISBN 9781949759259

THIS BOOK IS FOR YOU.

From my soul to yours.

I wrote this book from the deepest and most vulnerable places of my heart for the ones who need it most and the ones that didn't know they needed it until now. It's for the people that fall, and fall deeply for all the wonderful things there are to love in this world, even if they are left broken in the process, yet they would still do it all over again in a heartbeat. It's for those who believe in happiness and put their heart on the line for their chance to find it. It's for those who have ever put so much of themselves into another person that they have forgotten just how magical they are just as they are. This book is for you if you know how beautiful it feels to bloom, to grow, to love, and to become you again. This book is for you if you're still working on that. This book is for you, and I encourage you to feel, feel every thought that comes to you when you flip through the pages. This book is your reminder that everything you'll ever need you can find within yourself.

—*Charlotte Freeman*

YOU CAN

You can.
Even if you don't believe it.
Even though it doesn't feel like it right now.
Even in the toughest of times,
You can.

UNREQUITED LOVE

No matter how much you wish you could, you cannot control how another person feels and loves.

Just because someone fails to see your worth, it doesn't make them a bad person, and it doesn't mean you are unlovable. It simply means that they are not meant for you.

You should never have to spend your days and nights wondering if you are good enough for somebody. You are enough. You are more than enough for the right person.

Always remember that your happiness comes first. Focus on loving yourself, really loving yourself and you will see your value and find the strength to walk away from unrequited love.

Weeks, months, years will pass and you'll look back and wonder why on earth it took you so long to see that all along you deserved everything you always wished you had.

—*You don't love me and it's okay.*

THE LITTLE THINGS

Maybe the little things that you consider your weaknesses are actually the things that people treasure the most about you. Maybe you hate that you care too much…or that you wear your heart on your sleeve, but some people think that's the best damn thing about you. We all have different little things that make up who we are; we don't need to change those things, but we can choose who we share them with.

BECOMING

Be strong, be kind, be free. Do things that make you proud of yourself. Surround yourself with people who bring out your best qualities, and distance yourself from the people who do the opposite. Be true—true to yourself and true to your morals. Stand up for yourself. Don't let people take advantage of your kindness and soft heart. Don't take shit from anyone, and don't put yourself down. Believe in yourself and believe in your journey. Be good to yourself. Be unapologetically you. Embrace your imperfections. Accept the fact that when you grow, sometimes you lose people and that's okay. Celebrate your every success and learn from failure. And most importantly, never, ever let anything stand in the way of the woman you are becoming.

RARE ENCOUNTERS

Throughout life we experience many different kinds of friendships. On rare occasions, we encounter someone so special that we just know we met for a reason. These are the kinds of friendships that last forever no matter what city you live in or how often you speak, no matter how old you get or what phase of life you are in. It's the type of friendship that has no judgment and sticks by you even when you f*ck up. It's the kind of friendship that makes you understand unconditional love. Maybe you met your most special friend when you were 6 or 13 or 30 ... or maybe you are yet to cross paths. It happens at different stages for different people. But when it does, there is no greater comfort than knowing that this person will be right there beside you to share the happiness, the sadness, and everything in between.

Never, ever take these friendships for granted.

SELF-PROMISES

Let yourself be sad, let yourself be a mess. But promise yourself that you'll try a little harder each day. That's all you can do. Take it day by day. You'll learn things about yourself you didn't know; you'll learn that all this time maybe you deserved more. A beautiful thing happens when you give your heart time to heal itself. You become you again. You find happiness again, and when you do, you know it's because of how far you've come when you thought you'd lost all hope. And if that's not something to look forward to, then I don't know what is.

PRESENCE

The biggest mistake you could ever make
is to live your life like you'll get another chance
to experience all the beauty that surrounds you.

HEARTS LIKE OURS

Maybe we held on a little too long to the people who didn't deserve us because we had more good in our hearts than they did. Maybe we saw them for how they could have been if they had a heart like ours. But they didn't, and maybe they never will. Hearts like ours are special. They should be treasured, not broken.

CHANCES

You will never know if something is meant for you if you don't give it a proper chance. Whether it's a relationship, a new job, a new city, or a new experience, throw yourself into it completely and don't hold back. If it doesn't work out then it probably wasn't meant for you and you'll walk away without regret, knowing that you put your whole heart into it. That's all you can ever do. It's a horrible feeling leaving a situation knowing that you should have and could have done more. So find the courage to take that chance, find the inspiration to make your next move, and once you do, pour your heart into it and don't look back.

SILENCE THE NOISE

You are the one that gets to live your life.
No one else is living it for you.
So choose the path that feels right to you.
Choose the person who feels right for you.
Silence the noise and do what feels right for you.

BREATHE

We can be our own worst enemy sometimes. We often think or expect the worst because it's the easiest thing to believe when we don't believe in ourselves.

Instead of being your own worst enemy, be a little kinder to yourself. Give yourself the credit you deserve, and try to see the situation for how it is and not how you have created it in your mind.

Give your mind a little rest, beautiful. Save that brain space for new ideas and new adventures, for the things you love and the people you love.

Breathe in, breathe out. You've got this.

FALLING INTO PLACE

This weird and beautiful thing happens as you get older. You stop caring about people who would usually get under your skin, and you start to focus more on your own life and the things that make you genuinely happy. You stop being fixated on other people's achievements and find yourself thinking about your own goals and your own future. Maybe it's because you begin to realize that no one else but you can get you where you want to be. Everything just kind of starts to make sense. Everything aligns. Finally.

COMING HOME

Love yourself, but take it slow.

For love to bloom it requires time, patience, respect, understanding, and vulnerability.

Accepting your true self and falling in love with yourself is a process that cannot be devalued or rushed.

Note to self: I'm coming home.

IT'S TIME

That one decision you are too afraid to make
could be the very thing that sets you free
in the best possible way.

It's been too long, darling; it's time to let go.

PAUSE

Sometimes you just need to have a break
from the things that are stealing your sunshine.

It's okay to put yourself first.

AS IT SHOULD BE

Wait for happiness. I promise it exists. It might not feel like it right now, but one day you'll wake up and everything will feel right. You'll be content with who you are and where you're going. Life will make sense. You'll still have good days and bad days, but it's okay because you'll know everything is as it should be.

THE BEST IN YOU BRINGS OUT THE BEST IN ME

Relationships are about being more than just present with one another. They are about bringing out the best in each other. Too often we stay in a relationship out of comfort, out of fear of not finding something better, or out of what we think is love.

A relationship should never make you forget your worth. One day you will realize that all this time you deserved so much more, and when you do, you will never look back.

MY KIND OF LOVE

Here's to a love that is patient.

A love that is calm and feels no rush.

A love that can ignore the expectations and deadlines of society and enjoy the incredible journey at its own pace.

Falling in love more and more with each day and every experience.

OVER-THOUGHT

Sometimes things don't make much sense when they are circling around in your brain. You think about something over and over and over until you have created a whole situation that may not exist or ever happen. It isn't until you speak about it or write it all down that your emotions become clear. Stop overthinking and stop convincing yourself there is no one who will listen to the thoughts that go on inside your head. Chances are someone is experiencing the exact same feelings as you are. Overthinking is a vicious cycle that is hard to break. So speak up; try to recognize when you are overthinking, reach out to a friend and share what's on your mind. You'll find strength in sharing the things you worry about and comfort in the fact that you are not alone.

EMOTIONS

The thing is, everyone on this planet feels all of their emotions in their own way. Sometimes you won't agree with how someone feels or deals with a situation, just like some people won't agree with how you deal with it. It's important to remember this. It's important to remember that things won't always go the way you want them to, and while you may not have any control over the outcome, you can control how you react to it. Every human on this planet is different, and if you choose to, you can learn so much from understanding why we feel the way we do and why others feel the way they do. Communicate, listen, and learn. Don't forget that others may be suffering, too, just like you are. Maybe they show it and deal with it in their own way, that you don't understand, or maybe they don't show it at all.

HOME

Stop wasting your time with people who don't know what they want. Why choose to be with someone that isn't right for you when you can be with someone who can make you happy, someone who appreciates you, someone whose presence has this weird way of making everything feel okay? Choose to be with someone who makes you feel like you're home, whether they are right there next to you or a million miles away.

SELF-PRESERVATION

Focus on yourself first.
When you're at your best,
You can give your best.

YOUR PERSON

Some souls instantly click.
Whether you're lovers, best friends,
soul mates, or something else.
You accept this person for everything they are,
and they would never let you be anything
other than your beautiful, imperfect self.
Maybe that's how you know you've met your person.

CONNECTION

One genuine connection
can make you feel at home
in an unfamiliar place.

RUN FREE MY LOVE

Don't ignore that little part of you that tells you to keep going—the little voice in your head that's strong and believes in you even when you are doubting yourself. Don't run from that beautiful, vulnerable part of who you are. That's the part that will lead you to great adventures and magical opportunities. Let that little voice speak louder— you have too much passion and determination to hide your gift from the world. Run free, my love; unleash your beauty on this world, and don't stop until that burning fire inside your soul feels proud.

FEEL LIKE ME

When it comes to love,
it's not always about
how you feel about that person;
it's about how that person
makes you feel about yourself.

You make me feel like me.

IT'S OKAY

I want you to know that it's okay
to feel whatever it is
you're feeling right now.

SELF-RESPECT

I promise you that once you learn to respect yourself you'll suddenly stop seeing yourself through the eyes of people that don't value you. You'll learn to stand up for yourself and feel sorry for those who can't see all the light you bring into this world. You'll realize that you deserve better than the way they make you feel about yourself, and you'll find more strength in that simple fact than you ever will with them.

JOURNEY

Sometimes we tend to forget
that our current situation
does not have to be our destiny.

EMBRACE

We would all be a little happier if we stopped changing who we *know* we are deep down inside to live up to the expectations of who we *assume* others think we *should* be. The truth is, it's okay to be who you are; life gets confusing if we are always trying to be someone else to impress people that don't matter.

Embrace your true self and I promise everything will fall into place.

SIMPLY, YOU.

Stop worrying about what other people think of you and focus on yourself instead. Focus on what makes you happy; focus on what makes your soul feel at peace. You are your biggest commitment, so start loving your flaws, your awkwardness, your weirdness, your intensity, and your vulnerability. Life becomes so much more fulfilling when you are simply yourself. The world keeps spinning whether people understand you or not, so why not make this next trip around the sun about you?

FOUND

Maybe you don't find your forever.
Maybe it finds you.

NEVER YOURS

Please, don't be so afraid of losing people.
There is nothing more scary or lonely
than losing yourself trying to please people
that were never meant for you anyway.

SELF-TRUST

When you make a positive change in your life sometimes
it takes a while to realize that you made the right choice.
Be patient and try not to overthink it. Trust yourself and
trust that better things are coming your way.

Broken But Free

Thank you for breaking my heart
And showing me that all this time
I deserved so much more.

Energy Shift

Don't waste time trying to win back the
one that broke you. Save that energy for
the one that's going to appreciate what
they have found from the beginning.

HIATUS

When life starts to overwhelm you, take a break from the things making you feel anxious.

Whatever it is will be there when you get back to it.

And if it's not, maybe you're better off without it.

SELF-LOVE I

Love yourself today,
Love yourself tomorrow,
And every day after that.

SIGNS

Stop ignoring the signs.
Stop breaking your own damn heart.
Know your worth.

CLOSURE

Someday soon you'll wake up in the morning and the first person you think of won't be him anymore.

It will be you.

START

Stop saying you'll do it "one day" and just do it. At some point, you have to make the first move. You have to make all the things you plan inside your head happen. You need to start taking steps to get what you want, even if they are baby steps. It's time to start working on that life you have always dreamed of. Put the fear of failure aside and just start, because the one thing scarier than starting is regret.

Sooner or later, you have to start.

MAGIC

They say seeing is believing.
So, darling, look in the mirror
And discover all the magic in you.

RESILIENCE

Every experience, both the good and the bad, will eventually get you to where you are supposed to be. Every win, every loss and every mistake. Don't be afraid to fuck up, and don't expect success overnight. Get lost, then find yourself over and over again. Work hard, and always remember to enjoy the life you create for yourself.

IT'S YOU

It's all you.
It begins,
It ends,
with you.

SELF-LOVE II

Falling in love
Should never be an excuse
To lose yourself.

DREAMER

Dreams don't have to make sense to everyone
to be possible.

VERSIONS OF YOU

I want to know who you are in your most authentic state, because too many people are trying to be like someone else. I want to see the real you. There is something so refreshing about an individual that is comfortable in their own skin and so unapologetically their own person. The sun truly shines from people who embrace who they are in every way.

That's the version of you I want to see.
That's the version of you I want to know.

BETTER OFF WITHOUT YOU

Letting someone go doesn't always mean
that you don't love them anymore.
It means that you love yourself enough
to become the person you need to be without them.

LOVE LESSONS

Sometimes two people, no matter how hard they try to make it work, just aren't meant to be. Love can do strange things to you, but it shouldn't ever make you forget your worth. Trust me, when you least expect it, someone great will come along. Someone that will teach you all the things you got wrong about love. Some people are just here to teach us a lesson. We must not regret these loves, but be thankful for them. When you finally cross paths with the right person, everything will feel different. You'll just know. Be patient. Please don't settle for less, because you deserve the world.

FEELING IS HEALING

Let
yourself
feel
before
you
heal.

INSTINCT

Relax.

Stop overthinking. You can't possibly know how you are going to feel in a year or even a month.

All you can do is trust your instincts and do what feels right, right now.

Everything is going to work out the way it's meant to be.

Have faith in that.

EASY LOVE

I love you because
You give me space to breathe.
I love you because
You give me room to grow.
I love you because
You believe in me.
I love you because
You let me.

TRANSFORMING

You'll eventually reach a point in your life where you start to realize your own worth, and you'll find that you won't take shit from anyone anymore because you're strong enough to know that you deserve better.

WEIGHT

One day you will wake up and all of a sudden the weight of the last few weeks, months, or even years will be lifted off your shoulders.

You can't control when that day comes; all you can do is stay strong and trust that it is coming.

LIMITS

I know you may be comfortable where you are, or you might be scared of the unknown, but please promise me that you'll try something new. It's too easy to live on autopilot. There is so much more to life than the limits of what we know.

MINDSET

Your mindset is your most underestimated power.
You will never live a positive life
With a negative outlook.

DOUBT

You'll go through days where you think you have everything under control, and you'll go through days where you have no idea what you're doing. Don't let one bad day get you down. Self-doubt is toxic and doesn't get you anywhere. It does nothing but hinder your progress.

BE YOU WHILE YOU CAN

Don't get caught up in situations that make you forget who you are. Life is too short to be anything but yourself.

PURE FORM

Free yourself from what others expect you to be, and embrace who you are to the fullest extent. That's beauty in its most pure form.

BEGIN AGAIN

No matter how perfect we aspire to be, and no matter how many things we promised ourselves we would do, sometimes all the things we wanted to achieve just can't happen in one day, and that's okay. That's real life. So whenever you have a bad day, just pick yourself right back up—chances are you achieved more than you thought you did. Chances are you're just being hard on yourself. Tomorrow is a new day. Allow yourself to begin again.

INITIATE

Life is too damn short to live in a mediocre way. Wake up with a purpose and make the best of each day and your short time on this earth. Stop saying, "I'll do this when I have more money" or "I'll start when I'm more settled." Stop making excuses. What if I told you that all you need is what you have right now? That's all you need to just make a start. It doesn't matter if you're 17, 30 or 50—set your alarm for tomorrow morning and wake up with a purpose. Always give your best and live your best life. Don't let the years just pass you by, because we don't get another chance.

This is it.

FEARLESS LOVE

Never assume it's a weakness to give love as openly as you do. People may take it for granted or take advantage of it, but promise me you'll never change because of it. Some of the most amazing individuals you'll come across in this life are the kind that never let the bad change the good in them. So keep seeing the good in everyone and keep spreading your love without fear. The world needs more people like you.

KIND HEARTS

There is actually nothing more attractive than a kind heart that respects yours.

—Stop putting up with shit you don't deserve.

FULL HANDS

If you hold on too tightly to people who have already let you go, you won't have the chance to grab hold of all the beautiful things that are actually meant for you.

—Let go.

CALM LOVE

Love is the most peaceful emotion ever. Stop telling yourself that it's supposed to hurt. Or better yet, distance yourself from the people who make you question how you should be loved.

UNCERTAINTY

Be gentle with yourself. There is nothing wrong with having no damn clue what you're doing. Some of the best things in this life are built on uncertainty and taking a risk.

—Calm down, think less, do more.

TRUST YOUR JOURNEY

Don't be so hard on yourself for feeling lost, confused, or like you haven't achieved all that you wanted to achieve. Life would be boring if you'd done it all already, if you had no more room to grow or things to learn. Be patient. You'll eventually figure it all out, and everything will make perfect sense. Every experience will get you to where you are supposed to be. Every loss, every heartbreak, and every mistake. Don't be afraid to mess up, and don't expect success overnight. Get lost; get so damn lost and find yourself over and over again. Believe in yourself, forget about what other people think, and trust your journey.

RELAX

Please stop overthinking life like you have to have an answer to every feeling or situation. That's not how life works. We figure it all out by just living. By messing up, by missing an opportunity, by seeking advice and not taking it. We learn what's important and what isn't. Sometimes we have no damn clue what to do, and that's okay. Always trust your gut and know that everything works out the way it's meant to. It always does.

Relax; we were never in control anyway.

CLOSED DOORS

The truth is,
I don't think you'll ever understand
The extent of what I felt for you.
Or what I'd have done for you.
And I hate that you never gave yourself the chance
to let me show you.

SOUL "MATES"

I don't think some people realize how lucky they are when they find their soul mate in a friendship.

TIMING V. FATE

Maybe "bad timing" is a sign that perhaps this isn't right for you right now. Maybe this isn't meant to happen like this. Try to focus on yourself and do your own thing. If it works, it works. If it doesn't, it doesn't. When you find the one who is supposed to be in your life, you'll just know, you'll make it happen. You won't question the timing.

Maybe this just isn't it.

PACE

Just because other people are doing something, it doesn't mean that you have to. Go at your own pace. Remember that age is just a number and stop letting it define you. Find the freedom in creating your own timeline.

YOU ARE IN CONTROL

The thing about this way that you feel is that it's only temporary. I know that your mind is consumed right now, suffocating; it's like you can't find a way to think about anything other than the things that are causing you anxiety. These feelings don't last. It may not feel like it right now, but this feeling will fade; maybe not today, maybe not tomorrow, but you will smile again, you will feel like you again, you will feel happy and full of life again. Nothing is permanent. That's the bittersweet part about life. That's why it's so important to appreciate the truly amazing parts and people in your life while also understanding that the bad days won't last forever. Always be present, always be grateful, always know that you'll get through this obstacle and the one after that. You're so much stronger than you think you are right now. Think about it; you've gotten through every tough day in your life so far, and this is no different. Take a big breath and think of all the things you have to be grateful for and breathe out all the bad.

You are in control of how you feel.

You are in control of this moment.

SELF-LOVE III

Self-love can go a long way.
Self-love can heal you.
Self-love can save you.

ENOUGH

Some days you need to simply look in the mirror and say to yourself, "I did what I could today, and it's enough."

TOXIC LOVE

One of the hardest things about a toxic relationship is knowing when to leave. It's too easy to get stuck in the mindset that things will improve, that things will change. When you love somebody it's only natural to want to hold on, but you need to look at what this relationship is doing to you. Don't sacrifice your happiness for something that feels wrong. Love shouldn't make you feel unhappy; it shouldn't make you constantly question if the relationship is right or if it will work long-term. Doubt is a warning sign that too many people ignore. It's like your head already knows the answer, but your heart wants to hold on.

Maybe we do this because we are brought up to stand by the ones we love. Maybe it's confusing because there is no lack of love in a toxic relationship. These relationships feel so intense and so passionate—almost magnetic. It can take a long time, a very brave decision and a broken heart to release that magnetic force, to realize that you need so much more than love to make it work. You need trust, you need patience, and you need respect. It's okay to realize that maybe there isn't a future where you once hoped there was.

If you deny how you feel now it will come out in other ways over time. Know that it's okay to leave; it's okay to spread your wings and to grow. Trust that all the love you've been giving to the wrong person will find its way to all of the people who are meant to be in your life.

I know that leaving your comfort zone is scary, but if this relationship is putting out your light, you need to stand up for yourself and trust your decision. Don't let anyone else devalue your emotions and how this relationship makes you feel. There is so much more to life than a toxic, negative relationship. There is so much more love to discover; you just need to be brave. It's all in your hands now.

YOUR TIME IS COMING

Try not to compare yourself to people around you. Life isn't a race; it's about making the right decisions at the right time. Do things at your own pace; take less notice of what everyone else is doing. Don't be jealous of situations that you know little about. Don't be jealous when people around you reach milestones; be happy for them, be patient and know that your time is coming. Everything happens at the exact moment it's supposed to.

Us, Always.

I will always be me,
And you will always be you.
But as long as we are together,
It will always be us.

Grow

It's okay to leave,
It's okay to spread your wings,
It's okay to grow.

NO RETURNS

He broke you.
He knows he did, too.
Don't run back.
Please don't run back
Don't run back to someone
Who has no intention
Of being gentle with your heart.

PURSUE

If it makes you happy,
Pursue it.

HUMAN

Allow yourself to have a bad day
Without punishing yourself for it.
You are only human.
Please be kind to yourself.

PLANS

Things don't always work out the way we planned.

But you should never regret following your heart.

You should never regret going after what makes your heart happy.

REALIZATION

And then one day I realized
I was far more deserving of my love
Than the one who broke me.

YOU'RE NOT ALONE

You don't have to fight the way that you are feeling on your own. There is always going to be someone that understands what you are going through. Don't be afraid to reach out; I promise you're not alone in this.

HEART SET FREE

Don't let a broken heart stop you from sharing your love with the world. Keep being you, keep that big beautiful heart of yours open.

RISE

The sun will rise,
The sun will set,
Each day,
No matter what,
And so will you.

LOVE, ALWAYS.

It's love. That's what life is about.
From the minute you are born,
Until you take your last breath,
When you really think about it,
It's always been about love.

LEARNING

When it comes to relationships, people are always going to have an opinion. Sometimes they are right and sometimes they're not. But at the end of the day it doesn't really matter what anyone else thinks, because deep down your heart always knows if you are supposed to be with someone—your gut will know if something is not right. Maybe it takes a little longer for your head to get the message. It's hard when the people who care about you the most only want what's best for you, but every decision you make needs to come from your own heart. It needs to be made based on how you feel, not on how others feel. You'll work it all out and see everything clearly when you are ready to. Every relationship is a learning process—you learn about what you want, what you don't want, and what you are really looking for in a partner and in life. Sometimes you don't work it all out right away, and that's okay. Sometimes you end up getting your heart broken, and that's okay. Sometimes you make the same mistakes over, and that's okay, too. It's all part of the journey. You are learning, you are growing, you are blooming, and it's beautiful.

ALREADY WHOLE

Stop spending your time with people who make you feel incomplete. Don't let anyone make you feel like you need another person to make you whole. You are already whole.

BE FREE

To be free
You must first learn to love yourself.

SAVED

Saying goodbye hurt for a long time, but it saved us from each other. Saying goodbye set us both free.

BLOOM

No words can really explain
The way it feels
To feel like yourself
To be proud of who you have become.

INNER PEACE

How do you know when you've found inner peace?

When you stop trying to control the things you know you cannot control, that's how you know.

FORWARD FOCUS

Stop living in the past.
Stop living in fear.
Don't you think it's about time
You start focusing on yourself
And the person you are becoming?

SAFETY NETS

Don't take the special people in your life for granted.

You never know just how much you could need them one day. Some people will walk in and out of your life, but the special people will always stay.

UNEXPECTED

I was looking for me
When I found you.

HOLDING MY HEART

When I met you, it was different. I wasn't afraid to fall for you because you held my heart in a way it hadn't been held before. I trusted you with it. I gave it to you, but you didn't take it all for yourself. You knew how important it was for me to be able to love someone but not lose myself in the process.

Maybe that's how it's supposed to be. Everything feels equal, everything feels calm. Everything feels like something you haven't felt before—and you know you could go the rest of your life feeling this exact way.

BETTER PEOPLE

I don't think of you anymore, but I'll always remember
how much I have grown since I put the pieces of my heart
back together. I didn't like who I was with you,
but I learned so much in my healing.

We are both better people now.

MEANT TO HAPPEN,
BUT NOT MEANT TO BE.

Maybe we were just two people
Who loved each other
But were not meant for each other.

HOPE

I hope you find someone that makes you happy,
That makes you the best person you can be.

PASSAGE

This is all a part of my journey,
And I'm right where I am supposed to be.

SEEING ME

Don't change for anyone,
Wait until you meet someone
That couldn't imagine you any other way.

KNOW WHAT YOU WANT

Please don't take my heart until you realize what you are looking for. I have been through so much at the hands of others. Please, just be gentle with me.

US AGAINST IT ALL

I have no interest in a "me against you" love.
All I want is an "us against the world" love.

PURPOSE

Dreams keep you going.
They keep you alive.
They give your life a purpose.
Please don't give up on them.

LONGING FOR CHANGE

Losing yourself isn't always a bad thing. Sometimes it's a sign that you're desperate for a change. Maybe you need to get lost to discover who you're supposed to be and what you're supposed to do. Don't be scared of feeling lost; embrace it. You're always growing.

MUTUAL DREAMS

If you're brave enough to share your dreams with me, then I promise you I'll do everything I can to help you make them come true.

HURT

I know that they hurt you.

I know that you feel angry, upset, confused, and that your heart has been shattered. But please, if they have shown you that they don't care, then you must find the strength within yourself to move forward. Don't try to fix anyone who makes you feel like you're not enough.

THE DECIDER

Often we move on,
Not because we want to,
But because we have to.

LEARNING TO LOVE YOURSELF

Distance yourself from the people that make you feel like you're not good enough, even if it's your boyfriend or best friend—you know deep down in your heart if someone isn't good for you, so live your truth.

Don't say yes when you want to say no. Respect yourself enough to say no when you know you don't want to do something—trying to please everyone will only set you back.

Stop comparing yourself to other people. Just stop. Everyone has their own journey, and you could be comparing your life to someone you actually know nothing about. Live your own life at your own pace. Remember that you don't know what goes on behind closed doors, and you might be aspiring to be someone that may not love themselves or their life at all.

Let yourself feel before you heal. Try to understand all of your feelings and then accept them. If you need more clarity, try writing it down on a piece of paper. Know that it's okay to have these feelings, and don't punish yourself for it. Once you give yourself the time to understand your mindset, you will begin to heal.

Celebrate your wins, no matter how small. You may not have done everything you needed to, but you got through something you have been putting off for a while. Focus on the fact that you achieved something you have been avoiding, and save the rest for tomorrow. You did what you could, and it was enough.

Be kind to yourself. Don't put yourself down. Don't let one negative thought become the way you feel about yourself. Try to turn a negative into a positive; watch how quickly your mindset can change from actively trying to be more positive about yourself.

Take care of yourself. Go for more walks, find something that you enjoy, something that makes you feel good about yourself, and try and do it a few times a week. Try to turn old, bad habits into new ones that are good for you.

Think about the people you spend time with. Are they toxic? Do they bring you down? Do you feel like you are worth more than the way they make you feel? It might be time to evaluate the kind of people you are surrounding yourself with and align yourself with people that lift you up and appreciate you. Also unfollow people on social media that make you feel like you need to look a certain way or you are constantly comparing yourself to. It's called self-preservation, and it's powerful.

Learn to stand up for yourself. Take control of a situation when you feel like you are being taken advantage of. It might be uncomfortable at first, but once you start to stand up for yourself you will learn to respect yourself so much more over time.

Understand that loving yourself is a process. It's not going to happen overnight. Be patient with yourself, and give yourself the time you need to heal and grow to love who you are on the inside and on the outside. Don't let anyone stand in the way of the person you are becoming.

Moving Forward

Sometimes you may not
be able to forgive someone.
Make sure you move forward, though.
Always move forward.

On The Fence

There is nothing
That hurts the heart
More than a lover
Who doesn't want to commit to you
But can't let you go.

LIVE YOUR LIFE LIKE IT'S YOURS

It's okay to do things a little differently, it's okay to be a bit behind or on a completely different path entirely. It's okay to have different dreams for your life. It's okay to live a life that some people don't understand.

It's okay to live your life for you. It's okay to not compare your life to anyone else's and to create your own goals and your own happiness—whatever that looks like to you. We've only got one life; it's okay to spend it in a way that makes you happy.

LAPSE IN REALITY

Don't trust how you look at yourself when you are feeling down. You are beautiful and you are strong. Don't let a moment of weakness change that.

VALIDATION

Stop believing that you need to be in a relationship to feel validated. I would much rather be validated as my own person than validated as somebody else's person. Please don't get into a relationship until you can see your worth as your own person first. Another person should never define you, even if you are in a relationship. Be you because of who you are, not because of who someone else is.

RECIPROCATION

Wait for someone who wants you
As much as you want them.

SUNFLOWER

Sometimes in life you cross paths with someone who instantly makes you feel calm, refreshed, alive, and wholesome. They encourage your dreams and celebrate your wins without an ounce of jealousy. They just want what's best for you, and you for them; there isn't much more to it. They are warm and bright, loving and loyal. You can't help but feel authentically happy in their presence, like the best version of yourself.

—Thank you for being my sunflower.

WHAT COULD BE

Make sure you go for it. Make sure you go for what makes your heart feel alive and happy. If there's a part of you that will always wonder what could have been, you need to just go for it.

UNDENIABLE CONNECTION

True connection can't be forced—it's something that either comes naturally or doesn't come at all. That's why it's so important to be honest about how you feel. If you ever get the chance to experience a genuine connection, please don't deny it. You're one of the lucky ones. That feeling is rare; don't let it pass by.

REMINDER

Remind yourself that you are in control.
You are in control of how you think,
How you respond,
How you act,
Who you spend your time with,
And who you share your heart with.

ME AND YOU

I love the person I am
When I'm with you.
I love the person I am
When we're apart.
I love me as much as I love you.
And that's how I know.

CHOOSING NOW

Maybe in another life we will find our way back to each other. Maybe in another life we would have worked.

But I choose this life, I choose now. I choose to let go and find someone to love me how I deserve to be loved, in this life and the next after that.

THAT FEELING OF FALLING

I hope we never forget why we chose each other. I hope we never forget that feeling of falling—how special it was to fall for each other in the same way at the same time. I hope no matter what life throws at us, we never forget that feeling.

CHANGE IS IN THE AIR

Something is telling me to let go of the past.
Something is telling me to let you in.
Something is telling me a change is coming.
Something is telling me I am moving on.

CHOOSE YOURSELF

If you shift your focus toward yourself instead of the person who broke you, you'll realize that all along you had the power to choose happiness by simply walking away.

Be there for yourself.

Choose yourself.

TIMELY ATTRACTIONS

Everything you attract is better when you are patient. Everything you attract is better when you trust the timing of your life.

FEEL HOW YOU FEEL

Don't let anyone tell you that your feelings are invalid. Don't let anyone make you think that feeling deeply makes you weak.

You know what you want and you are strong enough to know what you won't tolerate. You're allowed to feel how you feel, and you're allowed to be upset when someone tells you otherwise.

NEW YOU

There is nothing greater than realizing how much you have grown. There is no greater feeling than that moment you realize the "new you" rose above a situation that the "old you" would have crumbled under.

STILL HERE

Think about how much you have been through.
Think about how strong you are.
Think about everything you have overcome.
You're still here.

—*Reminders for when you doubt yourself.*

FORGIVE

Make sure you forgive yourself
for the mistakes you made
when you were growing.
Make sure you forgive yourself
for the mistakes you made
before you knew what you know now.

THE ONLY WAY FORWARD IS YOU

Sometimes the only way forward is to say goodbye.
Sometimes the only way forward is to choose yourself.

THE OTHER SIDE

Don't ever blame yourself or feel guilty for your progression. Be brave enough to leave behind what you have outgrown. Something better is waiting for you on the other side of this.

MOMENT IN TIME

In that moment in time, I needed you, and you needed me.
Maybe that's all we were ever meant to be.

MOMENTARY

Don't force what isn't meant to be.
Some people are only supposed to be temporary.

DREAMER

She was a dreamer
She knew what she wanted
But she was too afraid to do it
And that was the only thing
Standing in the way
Of who she was
And who she knew she could be.

HURT & HEALING

You are hurting but you are healing. It's such a beautiful thing. You'll look back at this moment in your life and be so proud of yourself and how far you have come. Know that this feeling won't last and that you'll look back at this phase of your life and be so thankful for everything you learned about yourself.

SEEKER

Never settle for less. Not with your job, your friends, and especially not with your heart. Continue to seek what you are looking for and do not shrink yourself for the sake of other people.

—You deserve the best.

TOO MUCH

Thinking too much
Is both a blessing and a curse.

ON MY MIND

Sometimes I wonder if you think of me
The way I think of you.
I wonder if you're feeling
What I am feeling, too.

LIVE FOR YOU

Live for you. Live a life that makes you happy. If you keep putting the needs of others before your own, you'll eventually lose sight of all of the magical dreams you had for yourself.

PERSPECTIVE

Instead of feeling like you're behind, feel grateful for each setback you've had in your life and each lesson you have learned along the way. Be grateful for each relationship and what you were able to learn about yourself through falling in and out of love. Feel proud of how strong you have become from each time you were left to put the pieces of your broken heart back together. Be grateful that you learned that you will heal again no matter what you go through. Some people never find this strength. You should be proud that you learned how to recognize and move on from situations that are no longer good for you. You might *feel* like you are behind, but when you really think about it, everything you have been through has made you the person you are now. Your experience is your strength, and you shouldn't wish to change that for anything.

HANDLE WITH CARE

Please don't waste your time with someone
who has no intention of being gentle with your heart.

MENDING

Things can happen in this life that don't make sense. You might even ask yourself how certain things could happen to someone like you. As you navigate your way through life, it becomes clear that nothing is out of the realm of possibilities. While you can't control what life throws at you, you can control how you rebuild and rise above from the moments that turn your world upside-down. There is good and bad in life, and you can't let the bad hold power over the good. You are blessed in more ways than you might realize right now, and this is not the end of the road for you. There will be many more laughs and many more moments of pure joy surrounded by the people that love you. Sometimes you need to push through the tough times to truly appreciate the good ones. Your heart may be in pieces, but this feeling will not last; your heart will heal again in good time. But for now it's time to be strong, it's time to accept, it's time to feel, it's time to mend.

VACILLATE

Two of the hardest things to do
Are staying when you know you should leave
And leaving when you want to stay.

REMEMBER

You're more than this.
You're more than this feeling.
You're more than this.
You're more than this feeling.

EPIPHANY

Then all of a sudden,
One day it clicked.
Everything that hadn't made sense in so long
Finally made sense.
The years of uncertainty
Fell into place
Just like that.

LOVE LESSONS

Be with someone who puts in effort
to do the things you like to do.
Be with someone who
makes you genuinely happy.

Be with someone who knows that it's the small things that
make you the happiest.

Be with someone that understands
that your goals are just as important as theirs.

Be with someone that is generous
with their time and energy.

Be with someone that reminds you
that you are loved—inside and out.

Be with someone that makes you
feel important and appreciated each day.

Be with someone that listens to you.

Be with someone you can laugh with.

Be with someone that understands
compromise is part of a healthy relationship.

Be with someone who isn't scared of your future, but
excited about it.

Be with someone who helps you
be the person you want to be
and doesn't hold you back.

PATHS

Maybe someday,
In some way,
In a universe far away,
We will meet again,
And everything will be okay.

BE KIND

The thing about kindness is that we rarely realize the impact it has on someone that truly needs it. It's not difficult to be kind, yet to some people the world feels so cruel. So be kind to your family, be kind to your friends, be kind to the person who takes your coffee order, the bus driver, and so on. You've got a lot of kindness in you, and you never know who needs it most.

Just As You Are

You are more than enough
Just the way you are.

Worth

You are worth more.
You are worth so much more
Than the way they made you feel.

YOURS

You smiled.
And before you even knew it.
I was yours.

PRIORITIES

There is a huge difference between giving up and putting yourself first. Don't let anyone make you believe you're giving up when you're actually doing what's best for you.

FEEL

Let yourself feel. Feel every thought. Even if the way you're feeling right now may not feel right or rational. Trust the process of feeling and healing. The way you feel is an emotional state or reaction to a situation or experience, and everybody experiences a situation differently—therefore the way you feel about something might be completely different to how somebody else does. We have a lot to learn from the mindsets of others. Let the feelings trickle in and out of your mind. Be patient with your thoughts; and more importantly, do not punish yourself for the way you are feeling. Please don't ignore them, either; it's up to you to work out what your feelings mean and sometimes it can take longer than other times. Feelings can also be conflicting and confusing, but we all must feel in order to heal.

GROWTH

Isn't it weird how you can experience situations throughout your life that are so heartbreaking or stressful that you can't ever imagine being okay again? Then a few weeks, months, or even years later, you notice that the days go by without thinking about those times. You can laugh, you can smile, you can go about your day and realize that you're so much stronger and happier than you thought you could be ever again. Those bad times might always be in your mind, in your memory, or in your heart, but somehow you feel at peace with your past; and the memories that come back don't punch you in the heart like they used to. You realize that you are, in fact, as strong as everyone was saying you were at the time and that you would, in fact, get through what you went through. Isn't it amazing how much we can change, how much we can learn, and how much we can grow?

PROGRESS

Stop stressing yourself out by thinking you have to do it all at once. Breathe in, breathe out. You've got this. Make progress, even if it's slow. Slow progress is better than procrastinating. You'll be surprised at how much faster you can get things done when you give each task the time it deserves.

THIS IS YOURS

This is about you. This is yours. So do those things you've always wanted to do. Learn that language, travel to that country, save for that house. Become confident in your own skin, grow to love yourself, create your own happiness. Quit that job if it makes you unhappy, get that degree, meditate daily. Exercise more, step outside of your comfort zone. Drink more water, look after yourself, be more optimistic. Work on that side hustle, read more books, and always, always trust yourself and your decisions.

HUMBLE BEGINNINGS

Always stay humble.
You'll never give up
If you remember why you started.

THE POWER OF KNOWING

Please don't settle for someone if you're wondering if you'll ever be truly happy. One day you'll meet someone you won't have to question; you'll just know.

BOUNDARIES

Get more comfortable with saying no. If you always let people get away with the things that bring you down, you'll always have to deal with the things that bring you down.

RELEASE

Let go of the things and people that hold you back.

YOU

The most powerful thing
You could ever believe in
Is yourself.

BETTER THAN YOU IMAGINED

Remind yourself that your life can turn out differently than how you thought it would and still be better than you could have ever imagined.

SHE IS

She is strong,
She is perfect,
She is enough,
Just the way she is.

TRANSITION

One important thing to remember as you get older is that it's totally normal to go through phases of connection and disconnection. In phases of disconnection, it's common to feel isolated, lost, or alone. Things can change so much in your 20s and 30s. People start to settle down, move away to new cities, and do what they need to do to build their future. It's only natural to feel lost or alone when there is so much change surrounding you, and you can see your life changing from what it was to what it is now. Don't overthink these emotions—understand that it's all part of your ever-evolving journey. Understand that the way we process all of these changes is different for everyone. Understand that it's totally normal to feel all kinds of different emotions through this transitional period. And most importantly, know that no matter how alone you feel, you have so much support behind you.

RISING

You are not falling; you are rising.

GO EASY

Be kind to yourself. Let go of the bad days behind you, and focus on all of the good days ahead. Life isn't always perfect, and neither are we. There will be days that don't go as planned, and there will be days that exceed all of your expectations. It's about balance; it's about taking the good with the bad. You can only do your best and sometimes, regardless of the outcome, your best is just enough.

THAT SIMPLE

Sometimes two souls are just meant to be.
Sometimes it really is that simple.

THE ANSWER IS IN YOU

Everything you'll ever need
you can find within yourself.

SURPRISES

People can be surprising. Sometimes there is a lot more to someone than you originally thought, and sometimes there is less, a lot less. It's easy to make assumptions about people because of our own expectations and how we treat people or view the world. In reality, everyone is vastly different. People can only react to things in the best way they know how. Experiences change people; we grow and evolve as we get older and learn how to deal with many of the situations and emotions we encounter in our own way. Remember that not everyone has had the same journey as you and not everyone views life in the same way you do. Some people are extremely self-aware and empathetic, while others lack that entirely. Some people wear their heart on their sleeve and share every thought, and others are a complete mystery and you can never really tell what goes on inside their mind. It can explain why we get so hurt by someone and the other person has no idea, or how sometimes we can say or do things that hurt someone else without knowing. Your journey is unique; your journey brought you here. You hold the power to surprise people with your huge heart in the best possible way, no matter how many times you've been surprised in the worst possible way.

TRYING ISN'T FAILING

The only people who ever really fail are the ones who are too afraid to try. There is nothing shameful about trying something and not getting the result you were hoping for; it's better than never having the courage to give it a go. Try, try again. Don't let the fear of failure hold you back. Do not listen to anybody that says you can't do it, especially if that person is you.

BEAUTIFUL BEGINNINGS

Day by day it can seem like nothing ever really changes. It seems like you are sacrificing so much of your time and energy, yet staying in the exact same place. It's not until you look back to where you started that you realize just how far you have come, just how much you have grown, and just how much you have achieved. Every late night, every tear, every panic attack, the dark circles under your eyes, the self-doubt and the self-criticism along the way— all worth it to finally see just how far you have come. And if you can't see it just yet, don't give up, don't stop now; this is only the beginning, and beginnings are so beautiful. Not because they are easy, but because they are full of hope, hard work, possibility, opportunity, and anticipation of what's to come.

PASSIONATE

How do you choose between your
passion and what's best for you?

Oh, darling, your passion is always
what's best for you.

LIFETIME OF MOMENTS

How your life feels to you is far more important than how it looks to someone on the outside. It's easy to get caught up in life and follow a path that has been formed in our minds by nothing but the expectations of other people. That's why it's better to fill your life with all of the people and all of the things that make you genuinely happy, instead of the things that seem to "validate" your life to people that don't necessarily matter. At the end of the day, I promise you will look back and realize that the moments that were made up of the little things that made you genuinely happy are the moments that filled your life with the most genuine joy, meaning, and purpose.

NATURAL FLOW

Don't force relationships to happen, and don't beg people to stay. Let everything flow as naturally as it can. If something doesn't work, no matter how hard you try, chances are it isn't meant for you. Have trust in that and move forward.

TOO MUCH

The wrong people often take up too much space in your heart, which can often leave you feeling emotionally drained, like you have nothing left to give. It's the people who are meant to be in your life that leave you with pieces of your heart, too, for all the other magical things in your life, especially yourself. No one should have you entirely, that's not how it's supposed to be. If you give yourself entirely to someone else, that means you have nothing left to give yourself. Choose someone that encourages you to be "you," someone that lets you be more "you" each day, not someone that demands so much of your valuable heart space that you can't even remember the last time you felt like yourself.

SPECTACULAR

And what a shame it is
That you don't see the beauty I see
Whenever I look at you.

What a shame it is
That you don't see your magic.

What a shame it is
That you can't see yourself through my eyes.

Because the view from where I'm standing
Is rather spectacular.

DAYDREAM

If you spend each day dreaming of a different life for yourself, this is your reminder to make a start, even if it's small. Do something today that can change your tomorrow.

NEXT STEPS

Sometimes, the only way to truly be happy is to just let go of whatever is holding you back and see what comes next. Be brave and have a little faith, you've got this.

PEACE IN YOUR PAST

It's easy to look back and question decisions you have made in the past, but it's unfair to punish yourself for them. You can't blame yourself for not knowing back then what you know now, and the truth is you made each decision for a reason based on how you were feeling at the time. As we grow up, we learn and we evolve. Maybe the person you are now would have done things differently back then, or maybe you are the person you are now because of the decisions you made back then. Trust your journey; it's all going to make sense soon.

WHAT'S TO COME

No matter how hard it gets, trust that the tough times won't last forever. I know it's hard to see it now, but you will overcome this, and what's to come —and everything will be okay again. For now, find comfort in the fact that you are not alone in what you are feeling, you are not alone with what you're going through.

I promise you are not alone.

EVERYDAY MAGIC

Promise that you'll never take this precious life for granted —the sunrise, the sunset, the fresh air and the ocean. Hug the ones you love so tight and live like it's your last day on this magical earth. Appreciate this wonderful world we live in and all the special people you get to share it with.

THE BEST KIND OF PEOPLE

The best kind of people are the ones who aren't afraid to be their own weird and wonderfully imperfect selves. These people make people happy, these people are so rare and special. We need more people like this in the world, and that's why you shouldn't ever wish to be anybody but your weird and wonderfully imperfect self.

ALL YOU NEED

You are not too old.
You are not too late.
You are all you need.

AN AUTHENTIC LOVE

Real love doesn't hurt.
Real love doesn't make you feel inadequate.
Real love is enough.
Real love stays.

THE UNEXPECTED

Isn't it beautiful how you can part ways with someone you thought you couldn't live without, to then find everything you were always searching for in yourself?

SAVING YOU

You'll get through
What you're going through.
Even if
Your heart is in two.
You'll find the strength
To save yourself.
Because saving yourself
Is what you do.
Think of all the times
You've made yourself feel whole.
Now gather all your pieces
It's time to save your soul.

ALL IN YOU

You have the power to control your thoughts. You have the power to turn negativity into positivity. You have the power to turn doubt into hope. You have the power to turn fear into action. And that means you have the power to change your life.

CHARLOTTE FREEMAN is an author and graphic designer from Queensland, Australia, who writes pieces that resonate from one soul to another.